The English
Practical Grammar Guide

By Phil Williams

Visit http://www.englishlessonsbrighton.co.uk for more
information and regular ESL updates.

Published by Rumian Publishing
ISBN: 978-0-9931808-0-4

Designed by P. Williams
Illustrations by Bob Wright

CONTENTS

PREFACE

This textbook is for English learners at Intermediate and Advanced levels, and above. It provides a deep understanding of the English tenses, considering grammar and practical use. It is a guide to all the time-based tenses, including their non-time-based uses, which will help you to use the English tenses in different, and more natural, ways.

ABOUT THE AUTHOR

Phil Williams is an English teacher and writer based in Brighton, UK. He has taught in schools and privately, in the UK, the United Arab Emirates, Russia and the Czech Republic, and is qualified with a Trinity Certificate in TESOL, and a Trinity IBET (Business English). He writes for businesses and entertainment, and manages websites - including the ESL website, *English Lessons Brighton* (http://www.englishlessonsbrighton.co.uk).

Phil can be contacted via email at phil@englishlessonsbrighton.co.uk, if you have any questions or comments regarding this book.

ACKNOWLEDGEMENTS

This book would not have been possible without my many students who have helped me understand the difficulties learners have with the tenses. I would also like to thank Nicky Geiger for her in depth discussions of grammar and the book's style, and Marta Rumian for helping me test the lessons contained here. I also want to thank my many beta readers, who helped me to complete this book, offering valuable feedback and encouragement, especially Bill Davies, Cristina Firoiu, Indah Soenaryo, Lianata Sukawati, Polina Zemtsiva, Rasha Zrieka, Stephen Thergesen, Veerle Verlinden, Venicio Sales, Yasemin Ozkanli, Yesim Yildogan, and Zhanna Yesmurzaeva.

Much of what I know about the English language I have learnt from reading and writing practice, and through answering the questions of my students. Two grammar books that have also greatly benefited me are Murphy's *English Grammar In Use* and Parrott's *Grammar for English Language Teachers*. Both of these books cover a vast range of grammar points, and are worth reading (and owning).

INTRODUCTION

This guide will take you through the English tenses from Past, to Present, to Future, with each section covering four main forms (*Simple*, *Continuous*, *Perfect* and *Perfect Continuous*). There are initial notes on grammatical form, examples for each form to demonstrate use, and detailed explanations for both the rules and the practical uses of the tenses.

These explanations are designed to help you learn the specific English grammar rules for the tenses and to identify common (often more flexible) usage. The complexity of the tenses and their uses often arises from native English speakers' ability to bend the rules of the language. In many cases the rules give way to general patterns, which can be difficult to master – this book is designed to help.

What are the English Tenses?

Time in the English language is essentially shown using twelve distinct grammatical structures, referred to as the tenses: four for the past, four for the present and four for the future.

These twelve tenses can be used for many different purposes. Because of these different uses, they are often called aspects rather than tenses. For the sake of simplicity, this guide will discuss these different grammatical forms (aspects) as tenses.

The tenses tell us about the specific points in time of actions, events and states. These can be summarised with short grammatical rules, but (as is true with much of the English language) these rules have many exceptions, and do not tell the whole story.

1

This is because English in practical use is always changing, and English is spoken so widely that different uses emerge from different regions. It is also because over time English has evolved to be used in particular ways, with ingrained exceptions to even the most simple rules.

For example, the present simple normally represents a timeless fact, for instance *heated water boils*, but it can also be used to talk about conditions in the present moment, such as *I feel happy now*.

This guide is designed as a complete comparison of the tenses to help explain where these exceptions emerge, why certain tenses can be used in different ways, and how to choose between similar uses.

How to use this book

This guide offers explanations of form, examples of form and explanations of comparative uses for each tense. You can read the sections individually to learn about different aspects of English, or you can read the book in order, to get an overall understanding of the tenses. The guide is designed to be read in full, but you may choose to use it for reference.

The guide begins with an explanation of the general rules of Form, to show how the different tenses are constructed. Each section then presents the Affirmative (Positive), Question, Negative, and Negative Question forms of a tense, putting the form rules into practice with numerous examples.

Following the form examples, the different uses of each tense are explained, followed by notes on how the uses relate to other tenses. These parts will help you understand the unique functions of the tenses, so you can choose between the tenses in everyday use.

In many cases, this goes beyond the basic single-use rules you may find in other textbooks, to show both the pure grammatical purposes of the tenses and the other ways that native English speakers use them.

There are regular examples and illustrations to aid understanding, with a glossary of grammar terms and additional information in Appendix 1. The examples used are deliberately varied and often unconventional, so carefully comparing the uses and examples (including those in the form tables) may help test your understanding of the information offered here.

Please note that this guide is written in British English. Although some consideration has been given to the differences between British and American English, it may still contain regionally specific language.

Colour coding

This guide is colour-coded to highlight important grammar points, structure and examples.

- Listed examples are given with bullet points.
- *Italics* show examples within the main body of the text, or additional information in listed examples.
- **Bold black** is used for structure and form.
- Orange highlights grammar rules and words of importance.
- Blue words indicate other useful sections in the guide or online.

FORMING TENSES

The twelve tenses are formed using four basic grammatical patterns: simple form, continuous form, perfect form and perfect continuous form. These four structures can be adapted across the three times: past, present and future. For example, the present perfect and the past perfect are structured the same way, with the verb **to have** in either the present or past.

Beyond basic grammar words such as subject, verb, and object (given in Appendix 1), the tense forms are best explained using three important words with specific grammar functions: the bare infinitive, the past participle and the present participle.

1. Grammar Words

1.1 The Bare Infinitive

To understand what the infinitive form of a verb is, it is important to understand its root. The noun infinity, and the adjective infinite mean something that is never ending. The infinitive is also something that never ends, it always keeps its form. It is a verb form, preceded by the word **to**, which never changes, regardless of how it is used in a sentence.

> ➘ **to read** – I like **to read**. / He did not want **to read**.
> ➘ **to buy** – I am trying **to buy** a book. / She had been hoping **to buy** it too.
> ➘ **to walk** – We ought **to walk** in the hills.

To find the bare infinitive form, consider the following sentences:

> ➘ Do you like to walk on a sandy beach bare-footed?
> ➘ What is in a bare cupboard?

What is the meaning of *bare*? When you walk bare-footed, your feet are bare. Do they have socks on? Or shoes? No, they are bare. So what is in the bare cupboard? Like with the bare foot, it has nothing on it or in it. The cupboard is empty. So, what is a bare infinitive? The infinitive is still there, but it is bare. The bare infinitive is still an infinitive, without the word **to**.

> ➘ read
> ➘ buy
> ➘ walk

When the bare infinitive is used in a sentence, therefore, remember it is still an infinitive, it simply does not include the word **to**. So, like the infinitive, its form must never change.

It is important to understand this, because when a bare infinitive is used to form a tense, it is not affected by time or subject-verb agreement.

With the tenses, the bare infinitive is necessary when forming negative forms and questions for the past and present, using "do" auxiliaries, and for future tenses which use **will** or **going to**.

➘ Do you **want** some wine?

➘ Did they **go** to the zoo?

➘ Will we **be** on time?

➘ Is he going to **feel** better soon?

"Do" Auxiliaries

The "do" auxiliary is a helping verb, used to create past and present tenses.

➘ do	➘ don't
➘ does	➘ doesn't
➘ did	➘ didn't

The "do" auxiliary functions only to form a grammatical structure, indicating time and subject, and does not provide extra meaning. It should not be confused with the use of **to do** as a main verb (which means to complete or perform). Compare these two sentences:

➘ I did my homework.

➘ Did you finish your homework?

In the first sentence, the main verb, *did*, means "completed" in the past, while in the second sentence *did* is an auxiliary, used to create a question. In the second sentence, *did* forms the question and *finish* refers to the action (completed). *To finish*, to complete, comes after the "do" auxiliary as a bare infinitive.

In fact, the "do auxiliary" is always followed by a bare infinitive when a verb is required.

❯ Don't **be** late!
❯ Do you **want** some tea?
❯ He didn't **eat** meat.

As the verb following a "do" auxiliary is a bare infinitive, it never changes. *He didn't eat meat* is in the past tense, but *eat* does not change. This may look like *didn't eat* is a combination of the past and present – it is not. It is a "do" auxiliary in the form of **simple past + bare infinitive**.

Understanding the bare infinitive is essential for accurately forming the tenses, and many other English grammar constructions. It will help you avoid incorrectly forming verbs that follow auxiliary verbs.

Modal Verbs

The pattern used for the "do" auxiliary is also used for the future simple construction, **will + bare infinitive**. The bare infinitive is therefore also useful for discussing future time.

Other modal verbs, and auxiliaries, also use this construction, and require the bare infinitive, including *can, could, may, might, must, shall, should, have to, ought to,* and *used to*. While **do** and **will** are very important for the tenses, however, the other auxiliary verbs and their specific uses are beyond the scope of this book.

1.2 The Past Participle

The past participle is used with the verb **to have** to form the perfect tenses. It is the third form of a verb, ending **+ed** for regular verbs.

> ↘ I have **wanted** this book for years.
> ↘ She had **cooked** too much dinner.
> ↘ The committee had **hoped** to finish the meeting early.

There is no rule for forming irregular past participles, which may represent as much as half of the verbs in the English language. Irregular past participles must be learned individually.

> ↘ I have **been** to France.
> ↘ He has **known** about the party for two days.
> ↘ They have **thought** about the offer.
> ↘ I had **given** my pen away.
> ↘ We had **broken** the rules.

The past participle never changes. Like infinitives, past participles do not agree with subjects. The past participle is always the same, regardless of subject or sentence position.

1.3 The Present Participle

The present participle is used with the verb **to be** to form continuous tenses. It is usually formed using the root of a verb +**ing**.

➘ I am **reading**.
➘ He is **cleaning** the car.
➘ They are **eating** cake.

The present participle never changes. Like infinitives, present participles do not agree with the subject. The present participle is always the same, regardless of subject or sentence position.

➘ I was reading.
➘ She has been reading on the train.
➘ They will have been reading for too long.

2. Tense Forms

This section explains the overall rules for forming simple, continuous, perfect and perfect continuous tenses. These are explained for affirmative (positive) statements, questions, negative statements, and negative questions.

If you are already familiar with the grammatical constructions of the tenses, you may go straight to The Past.

Contractions

The forms for positive statements, questions and negative statements are not affected by contractions (for example *I am – I'm, we will not – we won't*), so contractions are not included in tables for these forms in this guide.

The forms for negative questions, however, are affected by contractions. This is important, because negative questions that are not contracted sound very formal, and the contracted form is a lot more common. Typically, in a negative question **not** is placed after the subject, but a contracted negative question has the full contraction before the subject.

      ↘ Are you not going to the party?
      ↘ Aren't you going to the party?

2.1 Simple Forms

The simple tenses are formed using a verb in simple form, for past and present, or with **will + bare infinitive** in the future.

Simple Affirmative Statement Form

Affirmative statements in the simple forms of the past and present use the main verb in its past or present form, with no additional verbs.

➘ I like chicken.

➘ She hated the play.

The verb is formed based on regular spelling patterns or irregular forms.

The future simple is formed with **will** or **to be going to** and the bare infinitive.

➘ He will buy a new watch.

➘ He is going to buy a new watch.

Simple Question Form

Simple questions in the past and present are formed with the "do" auxiliary. **To do**, in past or present form (*do, does, did*), comes before the subject and the bare infinitive comes after the subject.

➘ Do you like eggs?

➘ Did she enjoy the play?

Simple questions in the past or present using the verb **to be** can be formed without **to do**, by placing the verb **to be** (*is*, *are*, *was*, *were*) before the subject. These questions do not require a bare infinitive.

↘ Are you happy?

↘ Were they at home?

Future simple questions are formed using **will** instead of **to do** or **to be**. These statements can be formed with or without question words at the beginning.

↘ Will you buy a new watch?

↘ Will he be happy with this room?

Simple Negative Statement Form

Simple negative statements in the past and present simple are formed by placing **to do + not** (in past or present form) before the bare infinitive.

↘ I do not like eggs.

↘ She did not like the meal.

Future simple negative statements are formed using **will + not** and the bare infinitive.

↘ He will not buy a new watch.

Simple Negative Question Form

Simple negative questions are formed by putting **to do** (past or present), **to be** (past or present states or emotions) or **will** (future) before the subject and **not** after the subject. Negative questions can be formed with or without question words at the beginning.

↘ Do you not like this?
↘ Does she not want any more?
↘ Is it not cold outside?
↘ Will he not buy a watch?

If **to do** or **will + not** are contracted (*don't doesn't, didn't, won't*), the whole contraction goes before the subject.

↘ Do you not want to go?
↘ Don't you want to go?

Will or Shall

The future simple can be formed with either **will** or **shall**. If in doubt, use **will**.

Shall is less common in modern English (and even less common in American English). It suggests doubt, or a weaker form. Some English speakers also use **shall** as a more formal form.

In question forms, **shall** is only appropriate for offers or suggestions. **Shall** should only be used in questions after **I** or **we**, and not with other subjects.

➞ Shall we dance?

➞ Shall I open the window for you?

Shall is incorrect in other question forms, and cannot generally be used with question words. In the following examples, **shall** would be incorrect in place of **will**:

➞ Will you pass me that book?

➞ What will the weather be like on Monday?

Examples in this guide are given using **will**, not **shall**.

2.2 Continuous Forms

The continuous tenses, also known as progressive tenses, are formed using **to be** (past or present) *or* **will** (future) + **present participle**. The present participle, in all tenses, never changes form.

Continuous Affirmative Statement Form

For continuous affirmative statements in the past and present, **to be** must be in the past or present, and must agree with the subject (*am, are, is, was, were*).

- I am going home. (*present*)
- He was going home. (*past*)

For future forms, **will** and **be** (the bare infinitive of **to be**) never change.

- She will be going home. (*future*)

Continuous Question Form

Continuous questions are formed by placing the verb **to be** (past or present) or **will** (future) before the subject. Questions can be formed with or without question words at the beginning of the question.

- Are you going home?
- Were they driving yesterday?
- Will she be staying for long?
- What will he be wearing to the party?

Continuous Negative Statement Form

Continuous negative statements are formed by adding **not** directly after the verb **to be** (past and present) or after **will** (future).

➘ I am not going home.
➘ She is not listening to you.
➘ They will not be driving here.

Continuous Negative Question Form

Continuous negative questions are formed by placing the verb **to be** (past or present) or **will** (future) before the subject, and adding **not** after the subject.

➘ Is he not going home?
➘ Was it not raining hard?
➘ Will they not be performing tomorrow?

For negative questions, if **to be** *or* **will + not** are contracted (*isn't, aren't, wasn't, weren't, won't*), the whole contraction goes before the subject.

➘ Isn't it raining now?
➘ Won't they be playing football later?

2.3 Perfect Forms

Perfect forms are formed with **to have + past participle**, in the past and present, or **will + have + past participle** in the future. The form of the past participle never changes.

Perfect Affirmative Statement Form

For perfect affirmative statements in the past and present, **to have** must be in the past or present, and must agree with the subject (*have, has, had*).

> ↘ I have eaten all the cake. (*present*)
> ↘ We had gone too far. (*past*)

For future forms, **will** and **have** (the bare infinitive of **to have**) never change.

> ↘ She will have arrived by this time tomorrow. (*future*)

Perfect Question Form

Perfect questions are formed by placing the verb **to have** (past or present) or **will** (future) before the subject. Questions can be formed with or without question words at the beginning of the question.

> ↘ Have they gone home?
> ↘ Had Jane heard about the test before you told her?
> ↘ Why have you painted that wall green?
> ↘ Will you have decided by tomorrow?

Perfect Negative Statement Form

Perfect negative statements are formed by adding **not** directly after the verb **to have** (past or present) or after **will** (future).

　　↘　I have not seen this film.
　　↘　She had not phoned me back.
　　↘　They will not have finished the project by then.

Perfect Negative Question Form

Perfect negative questions are formed by placing the verb **to have** (past and present) or **will** (future) before the subject, and adding **not** after the subject.

　　↘　Have I not been honest?
　　↘　Had you not done that before?
　　↘　Will they not have been briefed before tomorrow's talk?

For negative questions, if **to have** or **will + not** is contracted (*hasn't, haven't, hadn't, won't*), the whole contraction goes before the subject.

　　↘　Haven't we tried this already?
　　↘　Won't he have gone by then?

Perfect tenses and connecting words

Perfect tenses point to specific times in relation to other events, so they are often joined by specific adverbs or prepositions.

The present perfect is commonly found with adverbs that concern duration or link the past to the present, for example *just, already, since, yet* and *for*.

> ↘ We have **just** seen a movie.
> ↘ You have **already** said that.
> ↘ I have been here **since** this morning.
> ↘ I have known that **for** three weeks.

The past perfect is often connected to another past event, so is commonly used with conjunctions such as *and, that, because, so* and *when*, or prepositions or adverbs such as *before* and *already*.

> ↘ It was cold **and** I had foolishly locked myself out.
> ↘ He had eaten **before** the party.

The future perfect is used to show an action will be completed by a particular point in the future, so it is usually identified by expressions such as *by, before*, and *after*.

> ↘ They will have come back **by** noon.
> ↘ Robert will have cleaned the house **before** they get there.

2.4 Perfect Continuous Forms

Perfect continuous forms, sometimes called perfect progressive, use **to have + been + present participle**, in the past and present, or **will + have + been + present participle** in the future. In all forms, **been** (a past participle) and the **present participle** never change.

Perfect Continuous Affirmative Statements

For perfect continuous affirmative statements in the past and present, **to have** must be in the past or present, and must agree with the subject (*have, has, had*).

> ↘ I have been thinking about you. (*present*)
> ↘ She had been working all day. (*past*)

For future forms, **will** and **have** (the bare infinitive of **to have**) never change.

> ↘ We will have been walking for hours. (*future*)

Perfect Continuous Questions

Perfect continuous questions are formed by placing the verb **to have** (past or present) or **will** (future) before the subject. Questions can be formed with or without question words at the beginning.

> ↘ Have you been waiting long?
> ↘ Had they been trying hard enough?
> ↘ Will she have been cycling all day?

Perfect Continuous Negative Statements

Perfect continuous negative statements are formed by adding **not** directly after **to have** (past or present), or after **will** (future).

- ↘ I have not been listening.
- ↘ Peter had not been living there for long.
- ↘ They will not have been hiking all morning.

Perfect Continuous Negative Questions

Perfect continuous negative questions are formed by placing the verb **to have** (past or present) or **will** (future) before the subject, and adding **not** after the subject.

- ↘ Have you not been playing that game all morning?
- ↘ Had she not been dancing at the time?
- ↘ Will they not have been working on the project all week?

For negative questions, if **to have** or **will + not** are contracted (*hasn't, haven't, hadn't, won't*), the whole contraction goes before the subject.

- ↘ Hasn't it been snowing for days?

Perfect continuous tenses and connecting words

Perfect continuous tenses are used to show duration, and are often associated with the words *for* and *since*, or with the question *How long for?*

- ↘ I have been listening to this show **for** hours.
- ↘ He had been driving **since** the night before.

  How long will you have been living here **for** by next summer?

THE PAST

Events, actions and states described by the past tenses are usually finished, or were interrupted in the past, and do not directly affect the present moment.

Using the past, you can talk about complete events, events that were completed before other events, and events that were ongoing or interrupted at specific times before now.

- ➘ Something happened.
- ➘ Something was happening at a certain time in the past.
- ➘ Something had happened before another past event.
- ➘ Something had been happening before another past event.

These different tenses give you the ability to explain the past in sequences, and help you to relate different past events to each other.

THE PAST SIMPLE

3. Past Simple Form

3.1 Past Simple - Affirmative Form

Subject	Verb	Additional information
I	liked	that class.
You	helped	me learn a lot.
We	planned	to visit Croatia.
They	dreamed	of a better tomorrow.
He	whistled	very loudly.
She	worked	all night.
It	sounded	horrible.
Martha	played	football.

3.2 Past Simple - Question Form

Question word	did	Subject	Bare Infinitive	Additional information
What	did	I	come	here for?
	Did	you	like	the film?
	Did	we	win?	
How	did	they	know	we would be there?
Where	did	he	go?	
Why	did	she	say	that?
	Did	that big dog	bark	at us?

Note: past simple questions formed with **to be** (*was, were*) do not require **to do** or a bare infinitive.

↘ Why was I so tired yesterday?

24

3.3 Past Simple - Negative Form

Subject	did	not	Bare Infinitive	Additional information
I	did	not	learn	enough.
You	did	not	tell	me about the play.
We	did	not	want	another drink.
They	did	not	know	how to open the door.
He	did	not	smell	very nice.
She	did	not	give	me her keys.
It	did	not	look	fun.
Joseph	did	not	win	the competition.

Note: past simple negative statements formed with **to be** (*was, were*) do not require **to do** or a bare infinitive.

➘ You were not quick enough.

➘ He was not a member of the club.

3.4 Past Simple - Negative Question Form

Past Simple Negative Questions without contractions

Question word	did	Subject	not	Bare Infinitive	Additional information
	Did	you	not	hear	me shouting?
How	did	we	not	pass	the test?
Why	did	he	not	see	her again?
What	did	she	not	take?	

Past Simple Negative Questions without contractions

Question word	didn't	Subject	Bare Infinitive	Additional information
	Didn't	I	buy	the right milk?
What	didn't	they	understand?	
	Didn't	he	pay	the waiter?
Why	didn't	it	rain?	

Note: past simple negative questions formed with **to be** (*was, were*) do not require **to do** or a bare infinitive.

➘ Why was I not in the meeting?

➘ Weren't you happy about the decision?

4. Past Simple Uses

The main use of the past simple is for completed actions, states or events. It can also be used to emphasise detail or to describe a time.

4.1 Completed actions

The past simple is mostly seen as complete. This means the action or state described has finished, and can no longer change, with no direct effect on the present.

> ↘ We walked the dog. *(a task that finished, independent of now)*

The past simple does not have to refer to an activity, it can also describe a complete or finished feeling.

> ↘ I felt sad when my dog died. *(at that specific time I felt sad)*

The past simple is often indicated by a past time, such as *last week, in 1982*, or *on Monday*. It may also be indicated by a time clause, often introduced by *when*.

> ↘ They went home **at 9.30pm**.
> ↘ **Last week** I learnt about the Great Wall of China.
> ↘ It was too bright **when** they turned on the main lights.

A time clause is a clause (containing at least a subject and a verb) which describes a specific time.

> ↘ He was happy when they gave him a piece of cake.

In the above example, the whole clause *when they gave him a piece of cake* is a time clause, representing a time (the moment that the cake was given to him), signalled by the adverb *when*. Time clauses are covered in more detail in Appendix 3.

4.2 Emphasising detail

The past simple can be used to emphasise detail. If the past simple is used when another past tense is possible, it stresses that the action was complete.

For example, the present perfect is usually used to discuss visited locations, because experiences in different locations continue to affect us *now*, and can be added to, such as *"I have been to France."*

If you say *"I lived in France."* it emphasises that you were there for a fixed, specific period of time.

Similarly, we use the present perfect to say *I have seen this movie*, because the experience affects our current opinion. But *I saw this movie last week* (past simple) emphasises the completion of the action. It stresses when you did the action, and that the action was finished.

> ↘ I have seen this film. *(I now have that experience.)*
> ↘ I saw this film last week. *(I completed the action at that past time.)*

You may use the past simple to stress that you completed a recent action. This may demonstrate insistence, for example if you want to emphasize who the subject was:

> ↘ I have cooked dinner *(now it is ready).*
> ↘ I cooked dinner *(not someone else).*

I have cooked dinner. / *I cooked dinner.*

As this emphasises the subject (who *did* the action), it may also demonstrate annoyance:

↘ I have washed the dishes.
↘ I washed the dishes again.

4.3 States

All of the simple tenses (in past, present and future) can be used to describe certain states (usually verbs relating to conditions, emotions, senses and possession).

In the past simple, states are completed in the past, and are commonly found with **to have** (usually showing possession) and **to be** (usually showing emotions or conditions).

> ＼ I **had** two cars. *(I now have a different number.)*
> ＼ He **was** very sad yesterday. *(We don't know if he is today.)*
> ＼ They didn't **understand** why the car would not start. *(At the time, they failed to understand.)*

The past simple does not always tell us the state finished, though – and it may represent an ongoing state, or a state that was interrupted. It simply tells us that the state happened in the past.

> ＼ She **seemed** happy when I saw her.
> ＼ The bathroom **smelt** very strange last time I was there.
> ＼ Your hair **looked** fantastic.

In these cases, the states were ongoing, and may not have ended, but it is important to use the past simple and not the past continuous here.

There are many common state verbs that use the simple tenses; they can be grouped to demonstrate states of mind (*suppose, think, believe, understand, know, want, love, hate, need, like, prefer*), existence or possession (*be, have, exist, belong, own*) and senses (*feel, smell, seem, taste, appear, look*). Learn these examples, and be careful to use the simple tenses for them, and it will become clear when similar verbs are appropriate.

This topic is also covered in Section 16.3 (States), and in Section 29 (The Present Tenses and States).

THE PAST CONTINUOUS

5. Past Continuous Form

5.1 Past Continuous - Affirmative Form

Subject	To Be (was / were)	Present Participle	Additional information
I	was	talking	to a lifeguard.
You	were	sailing	on a boat.
We	were	building	a new shed.
They	were	behaving	like children.
He	was	laughing	at her joke.
She	was	thinking.	
It	was	getting	dark outside.
Paul	was	cheating	in the exam.

5.2 Past Continuous - Question Form

Question word	To Be (was / were)	Subject	Present Participle	Additional information
	Was	I	talking	too loudly?
Why	were	you	watching	that terrible show?
Why	were	we	playing	that game?
What	were	they	doing	that for?
	Was	he	doing	his homework?
When	was	she	singing	in the park?
Where	was	the guard	taking	him?

5.3 Past Continuous - Negative Form

Subject	To Be (was / were)	not	Present Participle	Additional information
I	was	not	listening.	
You	were	not	reading	quickly enough.
We	were	not	going	back to the castle.
They	were	not	paying	for their food.
He	was	not	working	hard.
She	was	not	coming	to the party.
It	was	not	snowing.	
Trudy	was	not	making	any sense.

5.4 Past Continuous - Negative Question Form

Past Continuous Negative Questions without contractions

Question word	To Be (was / were)	Subject	not	Present Participle	Additional information
	Was	I	not	working	hard enough?
Why	were	you	not	listening?	
	Was	he	not	whispering	quietly?
How	was	she	not	scoring	more points?

Past Continuous Negative Questions with contractions

Question word	wasn't / weren't	Subject	Present Participle	Additional information
	Wasn't	I	cleaning	the car?
When	weren't	you	drinking?	
	Wasn't	he	crying	when you got there?
What	wasn't	she	saying?	

6. Past Continuous Uses

The past continuous is mainly used to describe temporary actions or events that started before a specific point in the past.

It helps show that the temporary action or event was either ongoing in the past, or that the action or event was interrupted. It may also be used for some narratives.

6.1 Temporary actions

The past continuous shows a past action or event that started before a specific time in the past. This is usually a temporary action, so even though it has not finished we know it occurs for a limited time (so it is not a general fact or rule).

The past continuous tells us that the action started but had not finished (it was ongoing) at a specific point in the past. It may tell us the action was simply ongoing, but it may also tell us when the action was interrupted.

➤ I was walking home at 3pm. *(The action was ongoing at that time – it started before 3pm.)*
➤ They were eating dinner when the phone rang. *(The ongoing action was interrupted – it started before the phone rang.)*

6.2 Ongoing processes

The past continuous may also be used for a repeated action or event, to emphasise an ongoing process. This may show a series of events or a progressive action which took place over a specific period of time. It is still considered a temporary sequence or process.

> ↘ Jane was reading all day. *(The action was ongoing over the period of a day.)*
> ↘ We were preparing every night for months. *(The action was repeated regularly over a period of months.)*

With verbs of frequency, this may also be used to emphasise general habitual actions. This is usually done in a negative way.

> ↘ I was forever waiting for her to do her make-up. *(It was tiresome.)*

6.3 Narratives

In storytelling, the past continuous may be used for background information, or to present an action or event that came before described events. This is generally done by showing a past simple event (often in a time clause) interrupting a background event in the past continuous.

> ↘ He was taking a bath when the police knocked on the door.
> ↘ She was riding the bus when she first saw him.

She was riding the bus when she first saw him.

Here, the process of her riding the bus began before the narrative event that is being described – the occasion that she saw him.

The past continuous can therefore be used in narratives by using temporary actions and ongoing processes in the context of a story.

> *We rang the doorbell. No one answered. We went to the window and looked inside. They **were sitting** there, silent. **Watching** the TV. I decided it was a bad time to ask them about the tree.*

In the above example, the past continuous actions were ongoing at the time of the story's main events (they started before the described narrative).

7. Past Continuous and Past Simple

The past simple and the past continuous should not be confused. If you need to choose between the two, remember the past simple shows a completed action but the past continuous shows the action was in progress (it had started).

╮ I walked home. *(An action that finished.)*
╮ I was walking home. *(An action that was started.)*

This is often simplified, to say the past simple shows something was complete, and the past continuous shows something was ongoing, but this can cause problems as the past continuous can also demonstrate interruptions, signalling the end of an action or event.

It is better to remember the past simple tells us something finished and the past continuous tells us something was in progress.

╮ The dog barked. *(We know it stopped.)*
╮ The dog was barking. *(We know it started in the past.)*

Another area that can cause confusion is when using states. For verbs showing states, for existence, possession and senses (such as *be, have, seem, look, sound*), the past simple is used, even for temporary or ongoing actions.

╮ I was happy before the phone rang. (***not** I was being happy*)
╮ He seemed angry when we saw him at 4pm. (***not** He was seeming angry when we saw him at 4pm.*)

Beware, though – there are some exceptions to these state verbs, where the continuous can be used, following the regular rules. For instance with *feel*:

╮ I felt sad yesterday.
╮ I was feeling sad yesterday.

In these cases the continuous tense usually puts more emphasis on the temporary nature of the state, or the process.

Such state verbs and their uses need to be learned individually to avoid mistakes.

THE PAST PERFECT

8. Past Perfect Form

8.1 Past Perfect - Affirmative Form

Subject	had	Past Participle	Additional information
I	had	spoken	out of turn.
You	had	learned	enough.
We	had	heard	it all before.
They	had	listened	attentively.
He	had	watched	the game carefully.
She	had	read	about Somalia.
It	had	gone	awfully wrong.

8.2 Past Perfect - Question Form

Question word	had	Subject	Past Participle	Additional information
	Had	I	seen	him before?
Where	had	you	been?	
What	had	we	done?	
	Had	they	been	there for long?
When	had	she	found	the time?
	Had	Ringo	fired	a gun before?
How	had	it	looked	before the war?

8.3 Past Perfect - Negative Form

Subject	had	not	Past Participle	Additional information
I	had	not	worked	hard enough.
You	had	not	been	totally honest.
We	had	not	brought	the correct wine.
They	had	not	borrowed	many books.
He	had	not	listened.	
She	had	not	won	the race.
It	had	not	been	a good year.

8.4 Past Perfect - Negative Question Form

Past Perfect Negative Questions without contractions

Question word	had	Subject	not	Past Participle	Additional information
Why	had	I	not	heard	of this book before?
	Had	you	not	seen	the film already?
What	had	he	not	given	us?
How	had	Nina	not	juggled	before?

Past Perfect Negative Questions with contractions

Question word	hadn't	Subject	Past Participle	Additional information
	Hadn't	I	revised	hard?
	Hadn't	we	been	fair?
Why	hadn't	she	helped	us sooner?
What	hadn't	the doctor	told	us?

9. Past Perfect Uses

The past perfect is mainly used to demonstrate a sequence of events in the past. In more complex narratives, it can also show past states and background information.

9.1 Past event sequences

The past perfect usually shows an event that was completed before another past event. It is therefore often connected to a past simple event, and is commonly used with conjunctions such as *and, that, because, so* and *when*, or prepositions such as *before* and *already*.

> ❯ I had left my book at home **so** I did not study in the cafe.
> ❯ He had put on too much aftershave **before** he went out.
> ❯ They had brought back so much fish **that** the whole house stank when we arrived.

In all of these examples, the past perfect event finished before the past simple event.

As is true with other perfect tenses, the past perfect often has a connection to, or impact on, the event that it is linked to. In all of the above examples, the past perfect affects the past simple event. If it did not have an impact on the connected event, we could use the past simple.

> ❯ I studied hard and went to lunch. *(With no connection between the two.)*
> ❯ I had studied hard so I passed the exam. *(One event influences the other.)*

If you said *I studied hard so I went to lunch* this creates a connection between the two events; in this case, going to lunch is seen as a result of studying hard, perhaps as a reward.

9.2 States

The past perfect may be used to show the duration or degree of certain verbs of state, even when a continuous tense may seem appropriate. These verbs are generally the same states that use the simple tenses instead of the continuous tenses (such as *be*, *know*, *understand*, *want*). The past perfect shows that these states were complete, or took place, before another past event.

> ↘ I had known about the problem for two days when the printer broke.
> ↘ They had been to France four times before the millennium.

This use of the past perfect is common with visited locations and gathered knowledge, which can affect a later action or condition.

States in the past perfect are often ended, or interrupted, by the event they come before.

> ↘ It had felt scary, but we performed the song well.
> ↘ She had wanted a pony for years before they finally gave her one. *(Her desire was interrupted by the gift.)*

9.3 Background information

The past perfect is used in storytelling to provide background information. Main narratives in the past are usually in the simple tense, so the past perfect can provide details of events that happened before the main narrative.

Jim arrived at the crime scene. He found a man who had been shot.

In this example, the main narrative follows Jim, and when he arrived. The man was shot before Jim arrived, so the past perfect is appropriate.

This use of the past perfect helps put the subject in a situation before revealing past information. It can establish past events, and add details which were not important enough to explain earlier, or it can help put events in order of discovery for the subject (for instance for tension).

➘ We talked for hours before I realised we had met before.

➘ I walked into the restaurant and immediately ordered the goulash. I had decided what I wanted on the way.

➘ Hannah went into the kitchen and was devastated to find that someone had eaten all the pie.

➘ The children opened the door and looked down the stairs. They flicked the light switch, but there was no light. Someone had removed the bulb.

10. Past Perfect and Past Simple

The past perfect is used to show that an event finished before another event, while the past simple only shows the event finished.

If the time that the event finished is not important, or is easily understood, it is often possible to use either the past simple or the past perfect.

> ↘ I had travelled for two miles before I ran out of petrol.
> ↘ I travelled for two miles before I ran out of petrol.

These sentences essentially tell us the same information, and would be understood the same way. Grammatically, the past simple is more concerned with results (the travelling finished, and the petrol ran out) while the past perfect links the actions (the petrol ran out as a consequence of travelling / the travelling finished *because* the petrol run out). However, practically, most English speakers would understand both sentences to mean the same thing.

In another context, however, the past perfect can show that one completed action had a significant impact on the action that followed.

> ↘ I ate three sandwiches before dinner. I did not want any more. *(Simple statements that may not be connected.)*
> ↘ I had already eaten three sandwiches before dinner so I did not want any more. *(This sentence shows a more direct influence from one action to the next, that I did not want more **because** I had eaten three sandwiches.)*

The past perfect can also emphasise that a past action was actively done.

➘ He walked to the house and saw that the window was broken.
➘ He walked to the house and saw that the window had been broken.

In the first sentence, the past simple only tells us the window's condition (*it was broken*). With the past perfect, we know that someone or something actively broke it (*it had been broken* – caused by someone or something).

The window had been broken.

THE PAST PERFECT CONTINUOUS

11. Past Perfect Continuous Form

11.1 Past Perfect Continuous - Affirmative Form

Subject	had	been	Present Participle	Additional information
I	had	been	playing	volleyball.
You	had	been	cycling	for hours.
We	had	been	trying	to get to sleep.
They	had	been	swimming.	
He	had	been	going	home at the time.
It	had	been	snowing.	
Jamila	had	been	going	slowly mad.

11.2 Past Perfect Continuous - Question Form

Question word	had	Subject	been	Present Participle	Additional information
	Had	I	been	talking	too loud?
How long	had	you	been	feeding	the ducks for?
	Had	we	been	waiting	all night?
	Had	they	been	listening	for long?
Where	had	he	been	hiding?	
	Had	she	been	riding	a horse?
What	had		been	going	on?

11.3 Past Perfect Continuous - Negative Form

Subject	had	not	been	Present Participle	Additional information
I	had	not	been	waiting	long.
You	had	not	been	telling	me everything.
We	had	not	been	dancing	very well.
They	had	not	been	running	in the park.
He	had	not	been	reading	enough.
She	had	not	been	listening	for long.
It	had	not	been	moving	correctly.

11.4 Past Perfect Continuous - Negative Question Form

Past Perfect Continuous Negative Questions without contractions

Question word	had	Subject	not	been	Present Participle	Additional information
Why	had	I	not	been	sleeping	all night?
	Had	you	not	been	living	there long?
Why	had	he	not	been	working	that morning?
	Had	the ostrich	not	been	running	to the river?

Past Perfect Continuous Negative Questions with contractions

Question word	hadn't	Subject	been	Present Participle	Additional information
What	hadn't	I	been	doing	right?
Why	hadn't	they	been	drilling	for so long?
	Hadn't	she	been	feeding	her children?
	Hadn't	the crowd	been	asking	for trouble?

46

12. Past Perfect Continuous Uses

The main use of the past perfect continuous is to show the duration of a continued or repeated activity that was in progress at a specific point in the past. It can also be used to show that a recently completed action, before another event in the past, was an ongoing process.

12.1 Duration of past events

The past perfect continuous can show the duration of an ongoing action or event that was either finished or interrupted by another event in the past. It is often used with prepositions such as *for* and *since* to show duration up to a specific point.

➘ I had been reading for hours when I fell asleep. *(The action was ended by falling asleep.)*

➘ He had been singing for months before he started to take lessons. *(The action was interrupted by the lessons, but continued.)*

12.2 Completed past processes

The past perfect continuous can be used to describe an event that was completed before a point in the past, emphasising that the action was ongoing, or a process.

➘ Everyone was very tired at the party. They had been working too hard. *(Emphasising the process of working, finished before the party.)*

➘ Her hair was wet because she had been swimming.

This is used when the process is more important than its completion. It often stresses activity.

> ❯ I had been running.
> ❯ He had been talking on the phone.

It can also demonstrate irritation, similar to ongoing processes in the past continuous:

> ❯ We had been waiting for hours.

13. Past Perfect Continuous and Past Continuous

Both the past continuous and the past perfect continuous can show an ongoing process in the past, sometimes for the same event, with only a subtle difference in meaning.

> ↘ I was washing the car when she phoned.
> ↘ I had been washing the car when she phoned.

These two sentences essentially give the same information, but the past perfect continuous emphasises that *washing the car* happened earlier in the past; which can show it had been going on for a certain amount of time.

The difference becomes clearer when we add a duration to the sentence.

> ↘ I had been washing the car for an hour when she phoned. *(The phone call followed an hour of washing the car.)*

It would not be possible to show this duration with the past continuous. When we add duration to the past continuous, it tells us the action happened at the same time as the past event.

> ↘ I was washing the car for an hour while she spoke. *(She spoke at the same time as I washed the car.)*

The past perfect continuous is therefore used instead of the past continuous to clearly demonstrate that the ongoing process or repeated action started before another past event.

Another example:

> ↘ I wrote about why he had been living there. *(He did not live there at the time of writing.)*
> ↘ I wrote about why he was living there. *(He was living there at the time of writing.)*

49

14. Past Perfect Continuous and Past Perfect

The past perfect and past perfect continuous can both show an action or event was completed before another action or event in the past. The past perfect emphasises the action was finished, whilst the past perfect continuous emphasises the process, or duration.

> ↘ I had cooked dinner for twelve people. *(Emphasis on the completion.)*
>
> ↘ I had been cooking dinner for two hours. *(Emphasis on the process or duration.)*

The difference is essentially the same as the difference between the past continuous and the past simple, with the added detail that these events happened before another past event.

THE PRESENT

The present tenses describe the current moment, past events with a relationship to the current moment, and timeless facts. These tenses bridge the gap between the past and present, and can also be used (with future times) to show what will happen later. This makes them more flexible than the past tenses, and more complicated.

They can show:

- ↘ Something happens generally.
- ↘ Something is happening now.
- ↘ Something has happened recently.
- ↘ Something has been happening before now, for some time.

These tenses give you the ability to explain the present moment, timeless rules, and the past and future in relation to now.

THE PRESENT SIMPLE

15. Present Simple Form

15.1 Present Simple - Affirmative Form

Subject	**Verb**	**Additional information**
I	like	dogs.
You	run	fast.
We	read	magazines.
They	smile	too much.
He	moves	strangely.
She	plays	piano.
It	looks	expensive.
John	dislikes	tomatoes.

15.2 Present Simple - Question Form

Question word	**To Do (do / does)**	**Subject**	**Bare Infinitive**	**Additional information**
What	do	I	need?	
	Do	you	like	pigs?
How	do	we	get	out of here?
	Do	they	have	your bank details?
Why	does	he	listen	to that music?
What	does	it	say	in the instructions?
	Does	the council	give	you benefits?

Note: present simple questions formed using **to be** (*am, are, is*) do not require **to do** or a bare infinitive.

- Am I in the right location?
- Why are you so strange?
- Where is it?

15.3 Present Simple - Negative Form

Subject	do not / does not	Bare Infinitive	Additional information
I	do not	like	that noise.
You	do not	belong	here.
We	do not	know	where to go.
They	do not	look	very friendly.
She	does not	cook	good food.
It	does not	seem	right.
This water	does not	taste	nice.

15.4 Present Simple - Negative Question Form

Present Simple Negative Questions without contractions

Question word	To Do (do / does)	Subject	not	Bare Infinitive	Additional information
	Do	I	not	look	good in this dress?
	Do	you	not	go	to school here?
Why	does	he	not	work	harder?
	Does	she	not	like	my artwork?

Present Simple Negative Questions with contractions

Question word	don't / doesn't	Subject	Bare Infinitive	Additional information
	Don't	I	bake	nice scones?
What	don't	they	understand?	
Why	doesn't	she	need	her bag?
	Doesn't	that dog	have	an owner?

Note: present simple negative questions formed using **to be** (*am, are, is*) do not require **to do** or a bare infinitive.

➘ Am I not qualified for this job?

➘ Isn't she that disgraced politician?

16. Present Simple Uses

The main uses of the present simple are to show general facts or to demonstrate the frequency of events that reoccur as a fact. It can also be used for states, commentaries, storytelling and spoken actions.

The present simple is also used for future plans, which is discussed from Section 33 onwards.

16.1 General facts

The present simple can be used for general facts. These are timeless (with no beginning or end), and are true at the time of speaking. This is most commonly applied to events that occur as a rule, or part of a schedule, to demonstrate something that is always true.

↘ Hair **grows**.

↘ When you heat water, it **boils**.

↘ All lizards **look** the same. *(Note: though the present simple presents something as a true fact, it can still be a matter of opinion!)*

For activities, such as hobbies, this use of the present simple demonstrates something happens as a fact, generally, as it does not indicate a particular time or event.

↘ I play golf.

16.2 Frequency of general facts

The present simple can be used to demonstrate repeated activities. As present simple repeated activities occur as a general fact, the present simple does not indicate a particular time or event, but can demonstrate how often something happens.

⤑ I play golf every Wednesday. *(A frequently occurring fact.)*

⤑ I sometimes study English. *(An infrequent but recurring activity.)*

These repeated activities do not have a beginning or end, even though they may specify a regularly reoccurring time (such as *every Wednesday*).

Repeated events in the present simple are typically joined by adverbs of frequency, such as *usually*, *often*, *always* and *sometimes*. These adverbs usually come before the verb.

⤑ Jane **usually** buys our milk.

⤑ Elephants **sometimes** sneeze.

To demonstrate schedules or specific times, a time may be placed after the verb, with frequency adverbs such as *every* or *most*.

⤑ I run along the beach **every** Saturday morning.

⤑ We meet in the town hall **most** afternoons.

Frequency can also be shown with a preposition and noun phrase, for specific times that use fixed expressions, such as *at the weekend*, or when talking about specific days or dates, such as *on the third Friday of the month*.

⤑ She works at the weekend.

⤑ They deliver papers on Tuesday afternoons.

Elephants sometimes sneeze.

16.3 States

As explained for the past simple, all of the simple tenses (in past, present and future) can be used to describe certain states (usually verbs relating to emotions, senses and possession).

In the present simple, these states may demonstrate general facts.

╶ I live in Brighton.
╶ I have a large family.

These state verbs can also demonstrate temporary actions or events (which continuous tenses are usually used for), particularly concerning possession or the senses. All the following examples are true as general facts in the present, but are not timeless:

╶ I have a chocolate bar.
╶ She doesn't understand the question.
╶ This apple smells strange.
╶ Your dress looks lovely.

It is important to use the present simple for these verbs instead of continuous tenses, even though they may be temporary.

Remember: there are many common states that use the simple tenses instead of continuous tenses. They can be grouped to demonstrate states of mind (*suppose, think, believe, understand, know, want, love, hate, need, like, prefer*), existence or possession (*be, have, exist, belong, own*) and senses (*feel, smell, seem, taste, appear, look*).

Learn these examples, and be careful to use the simple tenses for them, and it will become clear when similar verbs are appropriate. If you understand, for example, that you need to say *"It smells strange in here."*, then it will be clear that you should also use the simple tense to say *"This room stinks of cheese."*

16.4 Commentaries

The present simple is often used for running commentaries. This provides an ongoing narrative, describing events as they happen, which is especially common for sports.

Sports broadcasters and other live reports use the present simple to commentate on events in real time (now), to save time and create drama:

 ↘ Ronnie passes to Jim, he shoots, he scores!
 ↘ The ball hits the net, and she loses the point.

16.5 Storytelling

The present simple is regularly used depicting past narratives for informal storytelling. It can create a sense of immediacy, urgency or informal friendliness, so it may be used for dramatic or comedic effect. This is common in spoken English.

 ↘ "So I go to pay for my sandwich, and the guy asks me for two pounds – but I don't have any money on me!"

The present simple is also commonly used to give narratives of consumed stories, for example the plots of films, books and plays.

 ↘ The main character finds the diamonds, saves the girl and stops the baddie. It's great.
 ↘ She says she's seen something, and you don't know if it's in her head or not.

This is used to put the listener in the moment of the story. This technique is sometimes used in creative writing, as well as in spoken language.

You may also find the present simple in advertising and other texts designed to put the reader in a particular scene or state of mind.

➘ A hot summer's day; you feel the cool breeze as you slip into the warm embrace of the golden sand. A bird sings above you.

16.6 Spoken actions

The present simple is sometimes used when the action is completed as it is spoken. This is useful for verbs forming agreements, commitments, suggestions and advice: *promise, suggest, apologise, advise, insist, agree, refuse* and more.

➘ I promise to be there on time.
➘ What do you suggest we have for dinner?

This use can be applied to verbs that pronounce a change, known as performative verbs. These verbs are normally used for official announcements or in very formal settings. There are a limited number of performative verbs, including *pronounce, declare, baptise,* and *arrest.*

➘ I declare this supermarket open.
➘ I arrest you in the name of the law.

THE PRESENT CONTINUOUS

17. Present Continuous Form

17.1 Present Continuous - Affirmative Form

Subject	To Be (am / are / is)	Present Participle	Additional information
I	am	reading	about Italy.
You	are	talking	too much.
We	are	running	late.
They	are	behaving	very badly.
He	is	sweating.	
She	is	learning	quickly.
It	is	snowing.	
Lisa	is	coming	down the stairs.

17.2 Present Continuous - Question Form

Question word	To Be (am / are / is)	Subject	Present Participle	Additional information
	Am	I	saying	it correctly?
What	are	you	reading	about?
	Are	we	watching	the game at mine?
Why	are	they	standing	over there?
How	is	he	coping	with the heat?
	Is	she	eating	her broccoli?
Where	is	that cat	going?	

17.3 Present Continuous - Negative Form

Subject	To Be (am / are / is)	not	Present Participle	Additional information
I	am	not	driving.	
You	are	not	wearing	the shirt I gave you.
We	are	not	going	the right way.
They	are	not	doing	what I asked.
He	is	not	smiling.	
She	is	not	getting	any better.

17.4 Present Continuous - Negative Question Form

Present Continuous Negative Question without contractions

Question word	To Be (am / are / is)	Subject	not	Present Participle	Additional information
	Am	I	not	being	generous?
Why	are	you	not	listening	to me?
	Is	it	not	working?	
	Is	she	not	waiting	outside?

Present Continuous Negative Questions with contractions

Question word	aren't / isn't	Subject	Present Participle	Additional information
Why	aren't	we	watching	the news right now?
What	aren't	you	telling	me?
	Isn't	he	building	a new house?
	Isn't	the weather	starting	to calm down?

18. Present Continuous Uses

The main use of the present continuous is to talk about temporary actions that are happening (ongoing) now. It can also be used for processes of change, habits, and, informally, to express some temporary states. The present continuous is also commonly used to discuss future plans, which is covered from Section 30 onwards.

18.1 Temporary actions

The present continuous is mostly used for actions or events that have been started but are not yet finished. More simply: for ongoing actions.

The action or event must be taking place for a limited time (it is not a general fact or rule), and this includes the time of speaking.

> ↘ I am walking home. *(I am doing it **now**.)*
> ↘ He is busy studying that book. *(He is doing it **now**.)*
> ↘ Where is that cat going? *(The cat is going somewhere **now**.)*

The present continuous is often taught as something happening now, but it may be a repeated event or an interrupted process that takes place in a period of time including now. The time of the sequence may include now, even if the actual action or event is not currently occurring.

> ↘ He is reading a book. *(He is in the process of reading it, but is not necessarily reading at this moment.)*
> ↘ They are building a house. *(Gradually.)*
> ↘ We are learning to speak English. *(Maybe not at this moment, but over a period of time.)*

The action or event therefore does not have to be physically occurring now, but the speaker is talking within a current period of time.

"Where is that cat going?"

18.2 Processes of change

The present continuous can be used to describe a process of change, which is common with verbs such as *increase, decrease, become, develop, expand, get,* and *grow*. This can demonstrate a general change:

➘ Unemployment is rising.
➘ The weather is getting warmer.

It can also show something more specific, such as a personal or more short-term change:

➘ The music in Jane's room is getting louder.

These processes are usually temporary.

To see the difference between the present simple and present continuous when we describe a change, the important question to ask is does the process have a possible ending?

➘ Howard is getting fat. *(Temporarily, because he cannot get fatter forever.)*
➘ Howard gets fat when he eats chocolate. *(Timeless, because this is a general rule: every time he eats chocolate it happens. It is not a single event or a specific time.)*

18.3 Emphasis on repeated actions

Though the present simple is usually used to show the frequency of repeated events and habits, the present continuous can be used to emphasise a repeated action. This is usually because the action is repetitive, and the present continuous can stress irritation. It is often used with adverbs like *always, forever,* and *constantly.*

> ↘ I'm always washing the dishes in this house.
> ↘ They are constantly arguing.

In both of these examples, the present simple could also be used, for a more neutral, factual statement.

> ↘ I always wash the dishes.
> ↘ They constantly argue.

These simple sentences only describe the actions, while the present continuous adds a more negative emotion.

18.4 Temporary states

The present continuous is sometimes used, in colloquial English, to show desires, senses, appearances and related states, to emphasise that these are temporary.

For actions and events describing states and senses, it is grammatically correct to use the present simple, and learners of English should avoid the present continuous, as it will mostly be incorrect and can lead to serious mistakes.

However, do note that English speakers sometimes choose the present continuous as a matter of style, or to emphasise the temporary nature of the state.

➘ He's looking very smart. *(At this moment.)*
➘ I'm loving this burger. *(Said whilst eating, demonstrating it is temporary.)*

"I'm loving this burger!"

19. Present Continuous and Present Simple

Pay careful attention to the comparisons between the present continuous and the present simple that are shown in Section 18.

The main difference between these tenses is that the present simple is timeless whilst the present continuous is temporary (current).

> ↘ I read books. *(generally true, with no specific time)*
> ↘ I am reading a book. *(a specific book, an action which will eventually end)*

This is often simplified to the present simple is general and the present continuous is now, but, as already seen, specific uses for both tenses mean this is not always true.

If both tenses seem possible for a present action or event (excluding states), the easiest way to choose the between the two is to ask is it temporary? If the answer is yes, the present continuous should be correct.

> ↘ That dog runs very fast. *(A timeless fact, the dog is always fast when it runs.)*
> ↘ That dog is running very fast. *(On this occasion.)*

A source of confusion can come from the use of the present simple for states. The particular verbs used for emotions, senses and possession that the present simple is appropriate for must be learned, as using the present continuous will cause mistakes.

THE PRESENT PERFECT

20. Present Perfect Form

20.1 Present Perfect - Affirmative Form

Subject	To Have (have / has)	Past Participle	Additional information
I	have	read	about their rules.
You	have	eaten	too much.
We	have	gone	the wrong way.
They	have	understood	everything.
He	has	collapsed.	
She	has	said	enough.
It	has	stopped	snowing.
Rupert	has	gone	home already.

20.2 Present Perfect - Question Form

Question word	To Have (have / has)	Subject	Past Participle	Additional information
	Have	I	seen	him before?
Why	have	you	received	so many awards?
	Have	we	caught	the right train?
	Have	they	made	a new birdhouse?
Where	has	he	gone?	
	Has	she	flown	a kite before?
What	has		happened?	
	Has	the clown	done	a dance yet?

20.3 Present Perfect - Negative Form

Subject	To Have (have / has)	not	Past Participle	Additional information
I	have	not	showered	yet.
You	have	not	given	me my money.
We	have	not	brought	our books.
They	have	not	built	cars for years.
He	has	not	learned	a thing.
She	has	not	gone	anywhere.
The smell	has	not	faded.	

20.4 Present Perfect - Negative Question Form

Present Perfect Negative Questions without contractions

Question word	To Have (have / has)	Subject	not	Past Participle	Additional information
Why	have	I	not	tried	this wine before?
What	have	you	not	seen	yet?
	Has	he	not	done	his homework?
	Has	she	not	read	that book?

Present Perfect Negative Questions with contractions

Question word	haven't / hasn't	Subject	Past Participle	Additional information
	Haven't	we	been	here before?
Why	haven't	they	studied	this topic?
	Hasn't	she	made	any progress?
	Hasn't	it	got	warmer?

21. Present Perfect Uses

The main use of the present perfect is to demonstrate complete actions or events relevant to now. It can also be used to show duration, for certain states and for occasional events.

21.1 Events relevant now

The present perfect's main function is to discuss complete actions or events that affect the current moment. These events happened in the past, but have a direct impact on the present.

- ➘ I have parked my car in the road. *(The car was parked in the past, but it is in the road now.)*
- ➘ I'm not hungry, I've eaten already. *(The subject ate in the past, but is satisfied now.)*
- ➘ They have learned to dance. *(They learned in the past, but have the skill now.)*

21.2 States

Like the present simple, past simple and past perfect, the present perfect is used for certain ongoing states instead of a continuous tense, particularly to show existence, mental states and possession, such as with the verbs *to be, to know,* and *to have.*

Of these senses, the present perfect is most commonly used to talk about locations visited or information gathered.

- ↘ I have been to sixteen countries in Europe. *(I went in the past, but I may go to more –the experience is relevant now.)*
- ↘ We have known about their engagement for two weeks. *(We discovered the knowledge in the past, and know now.)*
- ↘ I have had a cold for two weeks. *(The cold started in the past, but I still possess it now.)*

In general, present perfect states follow the same rules as explained in Section 16, but with an emphasis on showing an action that happened, or started, in the past, but is relevant now.

21.3 Occasional events

The present perfect can be used to highlight something done in the past when we expect to do it again. In this use, an individual action may be considered complete, but the action is expected to continue (even if it is the first occasion of the action).

- ↘ I have used the new computer twice. *(I may use it more times.)*
- ↘ They have met five times. *(They may meet more times.)*
- ↘ This is the first time I have ridden a horse. *(Possibly the first of many.)*
- ↘ This is the fifth time he has read this chapter. *(He may read it more times.)*

21.4 Duration

The present perfect may show long-term duration, for a continuing action or event. This use demonstrates a specific timed duration up to the present, rather than an ongoing process.

➘ He has lived here for twenty years. *(As he continues to live here, the number of years will increase.)*

The present perfect is mostly used in this way when talking about states. However, it can also show the duration of frequent activities, when you provide a reference to time.

➘ We have met here twice a week since last July.

This is different to the present simple, which demonstrates that an action occurs frequently, without showing duration (as it is does not indicate a specific time).

➘ We meet here every Tuesday.

22. Present Perfect and Present Simple

When using the present perfect to discuss an ongoing, or present event, it is normally used instead of present simple to show duration, or to show the event may be repeated. This is common with the state verbs, which use simple tenses instead of continuous tenses.

For example, the present perfect is often used to show duration with the verb **to live**:

> ＼ I live here. (*Shows it is true **now**.*)
> ＼ I have lived here for two years. (*Shows **how long for**.*)

The use for repeated actions is also clear with **to be**:

> ＼ I am happy. (*Shows it is true now.*)
> ＼ I have been happy many times. (*Shows it has happened a certain number of times up to now.*)

Otherwise, the present perfect usually shows a completed past event, not a present event, so it should not be confused with the present simple.

23. Present Perfect and Present Continuous

The present continuous and the present perfect can both describe recent actions or events that started in the past but are relevant now.

The present perfect usually shows an action or event that finished in the past, but is still relevant, while the present continuous describes an action or event that is ongoing (it has started, and is continuing).

> ↘ I have watched that film. *(in the past, and the experience is still relevant to me)*
> ↘ I am watching a film. *(which has not finished yet)*

"I have watched that film." / *"I am watching a film, I'll call you back!"*

There can be confusion choosing between the two with ongoing or repeated processes. The difference is that the present continuous shows an ongoing action or event, while the present perfect shows the action or event is complete up to now, though it could possibly happen again.

> ➘ We are performing every Thursday. *(The performances are regular and ongoing.)*
> ➘ We have performed six times. *(The performances were completed in the past, but we might do more.)*

24. Present Perfect and Past Simple

The present perfect and the past simple can sometimes be used interchangeably, as they both demonstrate complete actions.

The important difference is that the present perfect demonstrates the action affects (or is linked to) something that is relevant now. The past simple does not demonstrate a link to the present.

> ↘ We washed the car. *(The task was finished.)*
> ↘ We have washed the car. *(It was recently done, and / or it is now clean.)*

The present perfect should be chosen instead of the past simple when the action either has a current or ongoing effect, or can still be added to. Otherwise, the past simple should be used for complete actions.

> ↘ She escaped from prison. *(A single complete action.)*
> ↘ She has escaped from prison and is running away. *(A complete past event that informs us of where she is now.)*
> ↘ She escaped from prison twenty times. *(A total number of completed actions, with no suggestion that it can be increased.)*
> ↘ She has escaped from prison twenty times. *(A total number of completed actions so far, which can be added to.)*

THE PRESENT PERFECT CONTINUOUS

25. Present Perfect Continuous Form

25.1 Present Perfect Continuous - Affirmative Form

Subject	To Have (have / has)	been	Present Participle	Additional information
I	have	been	listening	to pop music.
You	have	been	reading	very quietly.
We	have	been	driving	in the country.
They	have	been	cleaning	for hours.
He	has	been	missing	since Tuesday.
She	has	been	dancing	in the evenings.
It	has	been	growing	rather quickly.

25.2 Present Perfect Continuous - Question Form

Question word	To Have (have / has)	Subject	been	Present Participle	Additional information
	Have	I	been	talking	for too long?
Why	have	you	been	whistling	for so long?
	Have	we	been	watching	the news?
How long	have	they	been	doing	that for?
Where	has	he	been	going	wrong?
	Has	that wolf	been	standing	all this time?
What	has		been	happening?	

25.3 Present Perfect Continuous - Negative Form

Subject	To Have (have / has)	not	been	Present Participle	Additional information
I	have	not	been	learning	enough.
You	have	not	been	eating	healthily.
We	have	not	been	swimming	recently.
They	have	not	been	living	there for long.
He	has	not	been	working	hard.
She	has	not	been	skiing	yet.
It	has	not	been	getting	any easier.

25.4 Present Perfect Continuous - Negative Question Form

Present Perfect Continuous Negative Questions without contractions

Question word	To Have (have / has)	Subject	not	been	Present Participle	Additional information
	Have	I	not	been	teaching	you?
Why	have	you	not	been	improving	during this course?
Why	has	he	not	been	listening	to the radio?
	Has	she	not	been	waiting	for too long already?

Present Perfect Continuous Negative Questions with contractions

Question word	haven't / hasn't	Subject	been	Present Participle	Additional information
	Haven't	I	been	saying	it was a lie?
What	haven't	we	been	doing	right?
	Hasn't	this	been	getting	more difficult?
	Hasn't	she	been	wearing	strange clothes?

26. Present Perfect Continuous Uses

The main use of the present perfect continuous is to show the duration of an ongoing present action or event (either by showing the timed length of the action or by showing when the action began). It can also be used instead of past tenses, or the present perfect, to emphasise the process of a recent action.

26.1 Showing duration

The present perfect continuous is mostly used to show the duration of a present action, often found with prepositions of duration *for* or *since*, or the question *How long...?*

> ↘ I have been reading **for** an hour.
> ↘ We have been trying to learn this **for** weeks.
> ↘ He has been sleeping **since** yesterday.
> ↘ She has been training **since** two months ago.
> ↘ **How long** have you been watching TV for?
> ↘ **How long** has it been snowing for?

It emphasises that the action started in the past, and the duration tells us how long ago it started.

26.2 The process of recent actions

The present perfect continuous may be used to describe a past action that affects the present, emphasising the process instead of the completion.

↘ I can't drive; I've been drinking.

↘ I've been thinking hard about whether or not to take the job.

In these examples, we are not interested in the action finishing, just that the subject experienced the process.

The present perfect continuous can also often be used instead of the past continuous to show something happened recently.

↘ I was walking in the park. *(in the past)*

↘ I have been walking in the park. *(recently)*

27. Present Perfect Continuous and Past Continuous

In most contexts, the present perfect continuous and the past continuous demonstrate a significantly different meaning.

The past continuous makes it clear that the action or event was in the past, while the present perfect continuous usually shows the action or event is ongoing – or still relevant.

> ↘ He was thinking about joining the army. *(Before now.)*
> ↘ He has been thinking about joining the army. *(He is still thinking about it now.)*

These both show an ongoing process that started in the past, but the past continuous sentence ended (or was specific to a time in the past), and the present perfect continuous is ongoing in the present.

The present perfect continuous can, however, also discuss a process that just finished. When this is the case, the past continuous and the present perfect continuous may sometimes be used to describe the same past process. The difference is that the present perfect continuous shows that the past process affects the present. Sometimes this means that the only difference is how recently the action or event was happening.

> ↘ I was running all night.
> ↘ I have been running all night.

"I have been running all night."

The present perfect continuous would be more appropriate closer to the event – in the above example it would be appropriate in the night, in the following morning or the following day. It would also be appropriate when the effects of the action are noticeable; you could say *I was running* as a general description of a past event, but *I have been running* to explain, for example, why you are tired.

The further we get from the action or event, the less appropriate the present perfect continuous is.

28. Present Perfect Continuous and Present Perfect Simple

The present perfect and the present perfect continuous can sometimes have a similar meaning, particularly when showing duration for states.

◢ He has lived here for years.

◢ He has been living here for years.

Grammatically, the present perfect continuous emphasises the process of the action, and the present perfect emphasises the total time, but in some contexts the two meanings can be very similar.

The present perfect may also be more appropriate for long-term actions. For instance, it can sound better to say *He has lived here for decades.* but *He has only been living here for two months.* (as it shows a shorter time).

For continuing and repeated actions, the present perfect can be used for an occasional action, while the present perfect continuous is more appropriate for repeated, ongoing actions.

◢ I have read about plants. *(A number of times.)*

◢ I have been reading about plants. *(As an ongoing process.)*

This is similar to the differences between the present continuous and the present simple (see Section 19).

29. The Present Tenses and States

Demonstrating states is one of the most difficult concepts when choosing a correct tense, so the following notes will help you decide which tense is most appropriate in different situations.

The present perfect is used for states when we want to emphasise the duration of the state, for an action or event that started in the past.

> ↘ I have known about it for weeks.

The present simple tells us that the state is true now.

> ↘ I know all about it.

The present continuous tells us that the state is temporary and ongoing (and **beware**, this use is often grammatically questionable).

> ↘ I'm liking what I hear.

The present perfect continuous tells us the state is temporary and ongoing, but emphasises that it started in the past (also **beware**, this is not always appropriate from a grammatical perspective).

> ↘ I've been liking this new song. *(For some time, up to – and including - now.)*

Directly compared, the present perfect suggests completion, or a state that will be completed in the present, while the present simple shows a state that is true now. The continuous tenses show states that are temporary.

> ↘ I have felt better. *(in the past)*
> ↘ I feel terrible. *(now)*
> ↘ I'm feeling bad. *(Now, but temporarily.)*
> ↘ I've been feeling bad all week. *(Now, but temporarily, started in the past.)*

This is a general example to illustrate the differences. Be careful, because in the wrong context such a direct comparison will bring about mistakes – especially when using the continuous tenses for states.

If in doubt, choose the simplest option. It is easier to use the simple tenses more flexibly than the perfect tenses, and it usually sounds clearer.

THE FUTURE

The future in English is formed in more complicated ways than the past and present. It still has the four main aspects of the tenses, (simple, continuous, perfect and perfect continuous), with definable rules and patterns. However, simple future time can be expressed with unique future forms (based on the auxiliary verb **will** or the **to be going to** form), or it can be formed with present tenses and a future time. This makes the future tense more flexible to form than the past and present tenses.

Future time can demonstrate actions and events that will happen, and demonstrates how these future events relate to each other. For example, it can show:

- ＼ Something will happen later.
- ＼ Something will be happening at a specific time later.
- ＼ Something will have happened before a specific time later.
- ＼ Something will have been happening for some time later.

THE FUTURE SIMPLE

30. Future Simple Variations

There is no single defined future simple form, as there are four main structures to form it.

- will + bare infinitive (*I will go home.*)
- to be + going to + bare infinitive (*I am going to go home.*)
- present tense + future time (*I go home on Friday.*)
- present continuous + future time (*I am going home later.*)

All of these forms can be used to discuss future events. The first two forms are for events to be completed in the future, whilst the present tenses with future meaning are for events that are arranged or scheduled in the future.

- I will learn everything in this book.
- I am going to learn everything in this book.
- I have a test on Tuesday.
- I am learning about grammar next week.

The **will** and **going to** forms are presented in full here, to demonstrate their structure.

The uses of the future simple are linked, so these sections discuss all future simple uses alongside each other.

31. Future Simple "will" Form

31.1 Future Simple "will" - Affirmative Form

Subject	will	Bare Infinitive	Additional information
I	will	go	to the park.
You	will	be	happy.
We	will	watch	a new film.
They	will	like	our new cat.
He	will	get	better at the guitar.
She	will	make	more muffins.
The giraffe	will	walk	again.

31.2 Future Simple "will" - Question Form

Question word	will	Subject	Bare Infinitive	Additional information
	Will	I	understand	the film?
When	will	you	arrive	at the house?
How	will	we	find	the keys in time?
	Will	they	care	if we leave early?
How	will	he	know	where to meet us?
What	will	she	do?	
	Will	it	turn	a different colour?

31.3 Future Simple "will" - Negative Form

Subject	will	not	Bare Infinitive	Additional information
I	will	not	be	mocked.
You	will	not	have	any fun.
We	will	not	get	to the museum in time.
They	will	not	remember	this tomorrow.
He	will	not	use	the car.
She	will	not	eat	dinner with us.
It	will	not	matter	tomorrow.

31.4 Future Simple "will" - Negative Question Form

Future Simple "will" Negative Questions without contractions

Question word	will	Subject	not	Bare Infinitive	Additional information
	Will	I	not	get	wet?
	Will	you	not	have	any more dinner?
Why	will	she	not	pass	the test?
	Will	it	not	look	strange?

Future Simple "will" Negative Questions with contractions

Question word	won't	Subject	Bare Infinitive	Additional information
What	won't	they	do?	
Where	won't	he	go?	
	Won't	she	seem	out of place?
	Won't	the guards	let	him through?

32. Future Simple "Going to" Form

32.1 Future Simple "going to" - Affirmative Form

Subject	To Be (am / are / is)	going to	Bare Infinitive	Additional information
I	am	going to	learn	everything in this book.
You	are	going to	like	my new bag.
We	are	going to	see	my grandma.
They	are	going to	miss	the play.
He	is	going to	read	about Cairo.
She	is	going to	play	the piano.
The rat	is	going to	eat	the cheese.

32.2 Future Simple "going to" - Question Form

Question word	To Be (am / are / is)	Subject	going to	Bare Infinitive	Additional information
	Am	I	going to	need	a coat?
What	are	you	going to	say?	
	Are	we	going to	like	this film?
When	are	they	going to	repair	the boat?
	Is	he	going to	juggle	those chainsaws?
Where	is	she	going to	get	the money from?
How	is	it	going to	drill	through that wall?

32.3 Future Simple "going to" - Negative Form

Subject	To Be (am / are / is)	not	going to	Bare Infinitive	Additional information
I	am	not	going to	listen.	
You	are	not	going to	like	this.
We	are	not	going to	pay	for this meal.
They	are	not	going to	meddle	in our affairs.
He	is	not	going to	wear	that coat.
She	is	not	going to	do	the washing up.
It	is	not	going to	clean	itself.

32.4 Future Simple "going to" - Negative Question Form

Future Simple "going to" Negative Questions without contractions

Question word	To Be (am / are / is)	Subject	not	going to	Bare Infinitive	Additional information
What	am	I	not	going to	give	them?
	Are	you	not	going to	visit	your mother?
Why	is	he	not	going to	help	us?
	Is	she	not	going to	perform?	

Future Simple "going to" Negative Questions with contractions

Question word	aren't / isn't	Subject	going to	Bare Infinitive	Additional information
	Aren't	you	going to	feed	the pigeons?
	Aren't	we	going to	assist	that old man?
When	isn't	she	going to	be	at home?
	Isn't	it	going to	look	beautiful?

33. Future Simple Using Present Tenses

33.1 Present Simple for Future Meaning

The present simple for future meaning uses the same form as the present simple (see Section 15), it just requires a future time.

➘ The bus leaves **at 2pm**.
➘ He comes home **tomorrow**.

Future times are generally adverbials (adverbs or adverb phrases), or time clauses, so they should come either at the very end of the clause, or at the beginning (used to show emphasis).

As the present simple for future meaning usually shows scheduled events, it is less common to show future time with a time clause, as time clauses create a dependent event.

33.2 Present Continuous for Future Meaning

The present continuous for future meaning uses the same form as the present continuous (see Section 17), it just requires a future time.

➘ Richard is giving a talk **this Friday**.
➘ We are going on holiday **next week**.

These future times are usually adverbials, so they should come either at the very end of the clause, or at the beginning (used to show emphasis).

For the present continuous for future meaning, future times can be shown with time clauses, connected either before or after the main clause.

➘ When the boat is ready, we are sailing to Morocco.
➘ They are giving the book back after they have finished it.

34. Future Simple Uses

In general we divide the uses of the different future simple forms according to these patterns:

- ➘ The will future form is mostly used for unplanned actions or events, or to make predictions that are not based on facts.
- ➘ The going to future form is mostly used for planned future actions or events, decided future actions or events or logical conclusions.
- ➘ The present continuous for future meaning is mostly used for future arrangements.
- ➘ The present simple for future meaning is mostly used for scheduled future events.

However, there is some overlap between these uses, as the following sections will show.

34.1 Unplanned events

The **will** future form is normally used for an action or event in the future that has not been previously arranged. This may be because it has been recently decided, or because it is a response to new information.

- ➘ They will not move. *(They have recently made this clear.)*
- ➘ I'll answer the phone. *(In response to it ringing.)*

Exactly what makes a future event planned, and how recently the event was decided, may be a question of context.

34.2 Planned events

A future action or event that has been arranged, or caused, before speaking is normally demonstrated with the **going to** future form. Usually it is not used for recent decisions.

- He is going to visit his parents in Scotland. *(It is already planned.)*
- They are going to build a house across the road.

This can include events that we believe will be completed, even if they are not arranged or scheduled, because they are likely.

- The caretaker is going to clean this mess up eventually. *(We expect he will, because it is his job.)*

The distinction between a planned and unplanned future action or event can be unclear, or flexible, so be aware that **will** and **going to** can be used in similar ways.

34.3 Making predictions

The **will** future form can be used for predictions *not* based on evidence. These predictions are often based on opinion, so **will** sounds more personal, or determined. This can include guesses, judgements based on character or assertions of faith.

These predictions often use adverbs such as *probably* or *definitely* to show the strength of opinion.

➘ I will win this game. *(This shows determination, but it is not a known fact.)*

➘ The shop will probably lose money this month. *(A guess or estimate.)*

If you replace **will** with the **going to** form in these examples, the prediction sounds more definite.

➘ I am going to win this game. *(It is almost certain.)*

➘ The shop is probably going to lose money this month. *(It is likely.)*

Predictions demonstrated with **going to** are therefore similar to planned events. They are future events that we have reason to believe are very likely, or inevitable. It may be based on present or past evidence.

"It's going to rain all night."

34.4 Decisions

The future form of **going to** can demonstrate a predetermined decision, even if the event was not previously planned or arranged. The future form of **will** normally shows more recent decisions. The difference can be subtle; it can be useful to think of decisions as plans; **going to** decisions may be previously planned and **will** decisions are unplanned.

> ↘ We've run out of milk, I'm going to buy some more. *(A plan.)*
> ↘ We've run out of milk, I'll go buy some more. *(A spontaneous decision.)*

34.5 Arrangements

The present continuous for future meaning is used for future arrangements, for instance when you have bought tickets, planned a time to meet or are doing something on a particular date or occasion.

> ↘ I am visiting my parents this Christmas.
> ↘ They're meeting us this Tuesday.

These arrangements can be formal or informal plans. They simply show that a plan is already established. This makes the present continuous for future meaning flexible.

Future statements in the present continuous that demonstrate arrangements are different to **will** and **going to**, which put emphasis on the decision.

> ↘ I am meeting with Charlene tomorrow. *(It is arranged.)*
> ↘ I am going to meet with Charlene tomorrow. *(I have already decided/planned it.)*
> ↘ I will meet with Charlene tomorrow. *(I just decided.)*

34.6 Scheduled events

The **present simple for future meaning** describes future events that are **securely planned**, for instance on a timetable or schedule. It is often used for the times of transport and events.

Though any present verb is possible, common verbs for this meaning are *start, begin, go, leave, finish, arrive,* and *come*.

> ↘ I have a meeting at 4pm.
> ↘ The train leaves at noon.
> ↘ They arrive tomorrow.

Similar to the present simple for present meaning, these future statements sound like secure facts.

34.7 "To go" and "to come"

The **present continuous for future meaning** is often used instead of **going to** for **to come** and **to go**, as people do not like to say going to go or going to come. This makes the sentence simpler. Compare:

> ↘ I'm going to the cinema later.
> ↘ I'm going to go to the cinema later.

This does not change the meaning, so the present continuous can be used for the **going to** uses (such as logical conclusions and secure decisions) for these verbs.

35. Comparing Aspects of the Future Simple

The four choices of future simple can be used in similar ways. You may hear a native English speaker use all four to answer the same question. For example, if asked *When are you going?*

> ↘ I will leave at 4pm.
> ↘ I'm going to leave at 4pm.
> ↘ I leave at 4pm today.
> ↘ I'm leaving at 4pm.

As shown in Section 34, these sentences all have subtly different meanings, and learners of English should note there are grammatically appropriate times to use each form.

> ↘ I will leave at 4pm. *(I just decided.)*
> ↘ I'm going to leave at 4pm. *(I decided earlier.)*
> ↘ I leave at 4pm today. *(as part of a fixed schedule)*
> ↘ I'm leaving at 4pm. *(as an arrangement)*

For an English speaker, in certain circumstances these differences may not be important, and the choice between the future simple forms may be taken as a matter of style or preference. Even if the particular uses become flexible, however, there are considerations that help separate the different future simple forms.

35.1 Formality

The present simple is the most formal simple future form, for definite schedules and timetables. In the example above, it is an exception, as *I leave at 4pm* suggests something regular, definite, or done as a rule. If it is not a regular, or rule-based event, the present simple is usually not appropriate.

The **will** and **going to** forms are also more formal than the present continuous. The future simple form of **will** can suggest determination (used for emphasis) while **going to** suggests a plan (used for predictions based on logic or evidence).

> ↘ I will finish this book this afternoon. *(I am determined to do it.)*
> ↘ I am going to finish this book this afternoon. *(I am certain.)*

The present continuous is the least formal, used for plans and arrangements that are set, and likely, but which can be either firm or casual.

> ↘ I'm walking home this evening.
> ↘ The doctor is seeing me at 10am.

Thanks to these more casual uses, the present continuous is very common in future simple statements.

35.2 Decisions

The future simple forms can be used to put different emphasis on decisions. The present simple should **not** be used for future events based on decisions, while the other three forms have subtle differences, which are worth repeating:

⤍ I am going to buy a new watch. *(I already decided.)*

⤍ I will buy a new watch. *(I decided recently, or am simply determined.)*

⤍ I am buying a new watch on Tuesday. *(I have arranged it.)*

These differences mean **going to** and the present continuous are often used for future events that are decided or arranged in advance; **will** is used for more recent decisions.

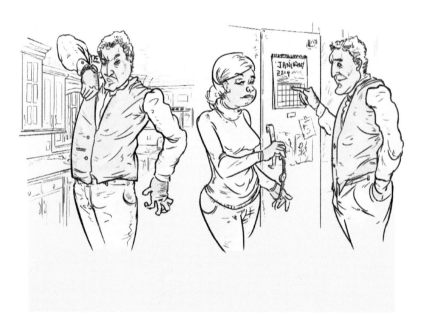

"I'll buy a new watch." /　　　*"I'm buying a new watch on Tuesday."*

35.3 Predictions

The future form of **going to** is the most common form for predictions based on fact.

The future simple form with **will** is used for more emotional predictions, emphasising an opinion or warning.

> ↘ It's going to rain later, it said so on the news.
> ↘ I think it will rain later, take an umbrella.

The present simple and present continuous are **not** appropriate for predictions.

35.4 Regular events

The present simple is the most appropriate future simple form for regular events. It may demonstrate one specific future event, but it suggests it happens regularly. The other three forms suggest we only know it is true at a specific future time, possibly even as an exception.

> ↘ The train arrives at 4pm on Friday. *(It is scheduled, perhaps regularly.)*
> ↘ The train is arriving at 4pm on Friday. *(This time.)*
> ↘ The train will arrive at 4pm on Friday. *(This time.)*
> ↘ The train is going to arrive at 4pm on Friday. *(This time.)*

THE FUTURE CONTINUOUS

36. Future Continuous Form

36.1 Future Continuous - Affirmative Form

Subject	will or am / are / is going to	be + Present Participle	Additional information
I	will	be talking	with them after work.
You	are going to	be sitting	next to the Mayor.
We	will	be basking	in the sun.
They	are going to	be waiting	when we arrive.
He	is going to	be diving	all afternoon.
It	will	be snowing	until dawn.
Mary	will	be watching	from the audience.

36.2 Future Continuous - Question Form

Question word	will or am / are / is	Subject	going to	be + Present Participle	Additional information
Where	will	I		be working	next week?
	Will	you		be talking	with Carl?
What	are	we	going to	be doing	later?
Where	are	they	going to	be watching	the game?
	Is	he	going to	be singing	an opera?
	Will	she		be helping	rehome the dogs?
When	is	Gregor	going to	be performing?	

36.3 Future Continuous - Negative Form

Subject	will or am / are / is	not	going to	be + Present Participle	Additional information
I	will	not		be seeing	them on holiday.
We	are	not	going to	be needing	any more paper.
They	are	not	going to	be talking	with the chief.
He	is	not	going to	be making	any more toys.
She	is	not	going to	be working	late.
It	will	not		be moving	very fast.

36.4 Future Continuous - Negative Question Form

Future Continuous Negative Questions without contractions

Question word	will or am / are / is	Subject	not	going to	be + Present Participle	Additional information
When	will	I	not		be cooking?	
	Are	you	not	going to	be working	on it at home?
What show	will	he	not		be attending?	
	Is	the bus	not	going to	be stopping	on the way?

Future Continuous Negative Questions with contractions

Question word	won't aren't / isn't	Subject	going to	be + Present Participle	Additional information
	Won't	I		be researching	this all week?
	Aren't	they	going to	be flying	to Asia?
When	won't	she		be dancing?	
	Isn't	the number	going to	be increasing?	

37. Future Continuous Uses

The two main uses of the future continuous are to describe events in the future that are in progress or to describe neutral future events (passive, or indirect references to the future).

The future continuous, like the future simple, can be formed with either **will** or **going to**. Choosing between the two forms in the continuous is similar to the choosing in the future simple, though the two forms are more flexible in the future continuous; **will** can suggest unplanned, or less secure future events, while **going to** is used for more secure plans.

37.1 Events in progress

The future continuous describes events in the future after they have started. These are usually planned or scheduled, when we know that an action will be happening at a certain time.

> ↘ I'll be watching TV from 9pm onwards.
> ↘ We will be working in the office when they arrive.
> ↘ He is going to be flying home while we prepare the presentation.

These events are not necessarily interrupted. The tense simply highlights that an action will be in progress.

The future continuous often puts future events in a context. As it shows the action or event in process, there is less emphasis on completion and more emphasis on the details surrounding the action or event.

> ↘ She will be dancing in the dark.
> ↘ They are going to be eating on the beach when the tide comes in.

37.2 Neutral future

The future continuous can be used in a similar way to the future simple tenses to show general plans or arrangements in a neutral way. It is used to avoid suggestions of intent, prediction, decision or willingness, which the different future simple forms demonstrate. In short, the future continuous can be passive, and removes responsibility.

> ↘ We'll be meeting on the roof.
> ↘ I am going to be catching the 5 o'clock train.

These sentences avoids telling us anything about who made the decision or why; they are more passive statements.

38. Future Continuous and Future Simple

You may find English speakers use the future continuous in place of the future simple with no real change in meaning.

 ↘ I'm meeting Charles later.
 ↘ I'll be meeting Charles later.

The future continuous is used more colloquially here, to sound more passive. For native English speakers, in such a context, the future continuous can have almost no distinction from the future simple.

Grammatically, however, the future continuous is only really appropriate here to emphasise the process of the action, to demonstrate the action will be happening.

If in doubt, the simple tense is better for clarity.

The neutral future continuous may be chosen specifically to emphasise that the arrangement is casual, or that the details are unimportant.

 ↘ We will sit by the window.
 ↘ We'll be sitting by the window.

In the above example the first sentence can be seen as a decision, or a plan to sit in that location, while the second sentence puts more emphasis on the context (the setting of *sitting there*) than the decision.

Similarly, the future continuous is used in place of the future simple for actions in progress, to emphasise the process, or to show that the action will have started before a certain point in future time. The future simple normally tells us when the action will start, or emphasises that it is planned.

➘ He will be running at noon. *(He will start before noon.)*
➘ He will run at noon. *(He will start at noon.)*

He will be running at noon.   /   He will run at noon.

111

THE FUTURE PERFECT

39. Future Perfect Form

39.1 Future Perfect - Affirmative Form

Subject	will or am / are / is going to	have	Past Participle	Additional information
I	will	have	read	it all by the morning.
You	are going to	have	attended	the concert early.
We	will	have	juggled	many problems.
They	are going to	have	given	us everything.
He	will	have	laughed	his last laugh.
She	will	have	gained	their respect after the presentation.
It	is going to	have	finished	before the show.

39.2 Future Perfect - Question Form

Question word	will or am / are / is	Subject	going to	have	Past Participle	Additional information
	Will	I		have	finished	by then?
What	are	you	going to	have	done?	
	Will	we		have	helped	the children?
Where	are	they	going to	have	left	the books?
	Is	he	going to	have	mended	the fence?
When	will	she		have	cooked	dinner by?
	Will	it		have	gone	by tomorrow?

39.3 Future Perfect - Negative Form

Subject	will or am / are / is	not	going to	have	Past Participle	Additional information
I	will	not		have	learned	enough by then.
You	are	not	going to	have	changed	anything.
We	will	not		have	fixed	the car.
They	are	not	going to	have	walked	far.
He	is	not	going to	have	finished	the essay.
She	will	not		have	waited	long.

39.4 Future Perfect - Negative Question Form

Future Perfect Negative Questions without contractions

Question word	will or am / are / is	Subject	not	going to	have	Past Participle	Additional information
	Am	I	not	going to	have	received	my award?
What	will	you	not		have	read	by tonight?
	Is	he	not	going to	have	gained	weight?
Where	will	she	not		have	visited?	

Future Perfect Negative Questions with contractions

Question word	won't aren't / isn't	Subject	going to	have	Past Participle	Additional information
	Aren't	we	going to	have	danced	all day?
Where	won't	they		have	been?	
	Isn't	she	going to	have	swum	down the river?
Why	won't	it		have	been	completed?

40. Future Perfect Uses

The future perfect is complicated to form, but has one simple use: to view a completed action or event from a particular point in the future.

The event described is incomplete (or has not started) in the present.

> ↘ He will have read the book by tomorrow. *(But he has not read it now.)*

The future perfect is therefore used to describe something that will be complete at a certain point in the future.

> ↘ They will have learned everything by the end of the year.

It should not be confused with the other future tenses, as it is the only future tense that tells us a verb will be complete. The simple tenses can show intent to finish, but the future perfect shows something will be finished at a certain time.

> ↘ I will finish my book tomorrow. *(The action is planned to be completed at a future time.)*
> ↘ I will have finished my book tomorrow. *(The action will be completed at a future time.)*

THE FUTURE PERFECT CONTINUOUS

41. Future Perfect Continuous Form

41.1 Future Perfect Continuous - Affirmative Form

Subject	will or am / is / are	have been	Present Participle	Additional information
I	will	have been	learning	this for a day.
You	are going to	have been	reading	for hours.
We	will	have been	doing	this for ages.
They	are going to	have been	washing	cars for weeks.
He	will	have been	driving	all night.
She	will	have been	waiting	for days.

41.2 Future Perfect Continuous - Question Form

Future Perfect Questions

Question word	will or am / are / is	Subject	going to	have been	Present Participle	Additional information
	Am	I	going to	have been	working	for long?
Why	will	you		have been	increasing	their pay?
How long	is	he	going to	have been	studying	for?
How long	will	she		have been	reading	for?

Future Perfect Negative Statements

Subject	will or am / is / are	not	going to	have been	Present Participle	Additional information
I	will	not		have been	walking	very long.
You	are	not	going to	have been	living	there for long.
We	will	not		have been	waiting	forever.
He	is	not	going to	have been	dancing	all night.
She	will	not		have been	drinking	today.

41.4 Future Perfect Continuous - Negative Question Form

Future Perfect Negative Questions without contractions

Question word	will or am / are / is	Subject	not	going to	have been	Present Participle	Additional information
	Will	I	not		have been	cycling	all morning?
	Are	you	not	going to	have been	working	on a solution?
What	is	he	not	going to	have been	studying?	
	Will	the rate	not		have been	falling	for days?

Future Perfect Negative Questions with contractions

Question word	won't aren't / isn't	Subject	going to	have been	Present Participle	Additional information
	Won't	I		have been	answering	their questions?
Why	aren't	we	going to	have been	travelling	for longer?
	Isn't	she	going to	have been	calling	clients?
	Won't	it		have been	getting	better?

42. Use of the Future Perfect Continuous

Though it is a complex tense to form, the future perfect continuous only has one function. It tells us the duration of an ongoing or repeated action or event that is in process at a specific point in the future.

It is often used with expressions starting *for* or *all*.

> ↘ I will have been living in Brighton for two years next Spring.
> ↘ He is going to have been swimming for an hour when they arrive.
> ↘ They will have been working all night long.

In these examples, we are showing how long an action will have been in progress, at a point in the future, and we know it will continue.

Sometimes the future perfect continuous may be used to show that an action will have been in process without a specific duration, but note that even in these cases it is still demonstrating a duration of time. This is more common to demonstrate process verbs.

> ↘ Next summer there may be problems with the job market, as unemployment will have been rising. *(for a certain duration of time)*

43. Future Perfects and other Future Forms

Though both the future perfect tenses are complicated to form, their uses are very specific, and they are not very flexible for replacing the future simple and future continuous tenses.

The future simple tenses can be used for various decisions or to describe future actions, but the future perfect tenses can only be used to describe actions from specific points in the future – either when the action is complete (future perfect) or ongoing (future perfect continuous). They are used to highlight completion or duration at that specific point.

> ➘ I'll read it at 3pm. *(A decision/arrangement to do it at 3pm.)*
> ➘ I'll be reading at 3pm. *(It will be ongoing at 3pm.)*
> ➘ I'll have read it by 3pm. *(It will be completed before 3pm.)*
> ➘ I'll have been reading for two hours by 3pm. *(At 3pm it will have been ongoing for two hours.)*

The future perfect tenses are therefore only required in very specific circumstances, when specific times in the future are important. Otherwise, stick to the simple and continuous tenses.

44. The Future in the Past

When you want to discuss time from a different perspective, for instance to show a future time seen in the past, tenses must be backshifted. It can seem complicated to express future time in the past, so this chapter is included to help introduce such constructions and use.

Backshifting in general, including for past and present tenses, is explained in Appendix 4.

44.1 Future in the Past Form

Future time in the past is formed with either **would** or **was/were going to** in place of **will** or **am / are going to** (as used in regular future forms). Future time in the past cannot be formed with the present tenses for future meaning.

This usually happens after an introducing clause in the past (for example with reported speech).

Regular Future	Future in the Past
I will eat dinner later.	I said I would eat dinner later.
You are going to read more.	You said you were going to read more.
We will be watching a film.	We thought we would be watching a film.
They are going to be playing football.	He said they were going to be playing football.
He will have finished the essay.	He would have finished the essay.
She will have been living there for a long time.	She would have been living there for a long time.

The forms of **would** or **was/were going to** may be used interchangeably, though the differences of uses between **will** and **going to** for the future generally apply.

44.2 Future in the Past Uses

Future time in the past is used to show that in the past it was thought that something would happen in the future. That future plan or expected event may or may not have happened (or may still happen later).

> ↘ I thought I would travel to Africa at the end of the year.
> ↘ She was going to learn to dance.

This use of the future in the past may show a future event is yet to be completed, and was recognised in the past.

> ↘ This morning, he started to think he was going to fail his exam.

This example shows when he started to believe this future event (*to be going to fail*) would happen. He may still fail in the future.

Future time in the past may clearly show something did not happen, though it was expected to.

> ↘ She was going to keep the letter, but her father tore it up.
> ↘ The advert said they would perform at 10pm, but they were late.

These examples shows past future plans that were not completed.

Future time in the past may also show future events recognised in the past that were completed.

> ↘ I told you we would win the game, and we did.

This use usually emphasises that the completed result was predicted before it happened.

The future simple in the past, as in the above examples, is used for similar purposes to the future simple. For more complicated future times you can use other future tenses in the past, guided by the same rules for use in the future.

For example, the future continuous in the past can show that in the past it was thought an ongoing event would be happening at a specific time in the future:

> ↘ I thought I'd be watching TV at 9pm.

The future perfect in the past can show that in the past it was thought an action or event would be complete at a specific time in the future:

> ↘ On Monday we thought that by Friday the boy would have returned.

Note, the future perfect in the past is also used as part of second conditional statements. These is a specific construction that demonstrates a past possibility.

> ↘ If we had caught our train, we would have been home by now.

The future perfect continuous in the past can show that in the past it was thought an action or event would have been ongoing for a certain duration of time in the future:

> ↘ It was believed that the students would have been studying for over four years by the time they left university.

These uses can seem very complex, because to understand how they fit together you may need to keep at least three references of time in mind: the time that your statement is said, the past time that your statement refers to, and the future time that the past action or event referred to.

AFTERWORD

This guide is designed as an overview of the many uses of the English tenses. The tenses based on time cannot describe everything you may wish to say in English, though. As well as forming sentences relating to time, it is possible to use modal verbs, conditionals and other constructions to deal with probable time, and possible or imagined circumstances, which require additional study and rules. There are also many individual or idiomatic forms and expressions that can be used alongside these tenses for different meanings and circumstances.

As this guide demonstrates, the English language is very flexible, and though there are guidelines for how to use the tenses, there are also exceptions and less common methods of using them. Not all of these uses are agreed upon by English speakers. To learn the contents of this guide, and apply its lessons, think carefully about the way you choose different tenses, and when native English speakers use them, and you will develop an instinct for when it is appropriate to use each tense.

The details of this guide can only lay out rules and patterns to show you how English tenses work. Learning how to work this knowledge into your own language patterns takes time and practice.

If you are interested in learning more about the English language, please visit my website at:

http://www.englishlessonsbrighton.co.uk

APPENDIX 1

GLOSSARY OF ENGLISH TERMS

The following grammatical terms are important to understand this guide. This brief list should make the language of the guide clearer:

- **tense:** refers to one of the 12 grammatical aspects of time
- **subject:** the actor of the action or state, for example *you, the man, she, Charles, the building*
- **verb:** an action or state (doing/being) word, for example *walk, reading, lived*
- **infinitive:** an unchanging form of a verb, with **to**, for example ***to be***, or ***to read***
- **bare infinitive:** the infinitive without **to**, for example *be, read*
- **participle:** a word used as part of a verb form
- **past participle:** the third form of a verb, used to create perfect tenses, for example *walked, wanted*
- **present participle:** a word used to create continuous tenses, for example *walking, reading*
- **vowel:** the letters **a, e, i, o, u**
- **consonant:** letters that are not vowels, for example **c, l, s, d, n**
- **clause:** a complete grammatical phrase (usually containing at least a subject and verb). *The brown dog ate his food* is a clause, while *the brown dog* is not, as there is no verb
- **time clause:** a complete clause used to represent a point in time, for example *when the lesson ends* (see Appendix 3)
- **phrase:** a group of words that represent one idea, but do not link an action and actor, for example *the brown dog*

APPENDIX 2

ARTICLES AND THE TENSES

The definite article (the) is often used to refer to a tense, for example *the present perfect*. You do not always need to say tense, as it is usually clear in the context that it is a tense.

An article is not always necessary when the tense is used as an adjective or for naming purposes, for instance *present perfect questions* or *present simple exercises*.

Note that the tenses should not typically be titled with capital letters - I have used capital letters in the chapter headings and subheadings, as they are titles.

APPENDIX 3

TIME CLAUSES

Time clauses are used in English to demonstrate a period of time based on an action or event, similar to dependent clauses in conditional sentences. These are clauses that reference a point of time based on an action or event.

➘   I will cook dinner when I get home.

The clause *when I get home* represents a specific time (like *7pm, at noon, at night*).

Time clauses are complete ideas that require subjects, verbs and objects, but they do not always use the same verb rules as the main clause.

Identifying a time clause

Time clauses usually follow adverbs or adverb phrases that show they represent a time. These include *when, after, until, as soon as,* and *before.* A clause starting with an adverb of time like this creates a sentence fragment.

➘   When the sun sets…
➘   Before the first lesson…
➘   After my teacher arrives…

Although they have a subject, verb and object, none of these examples are complete sentences, they are times.

This is because when we use a time clause, the adverb of time links it to the main clause in a dependent way. Without the adverb of time, the two clauses could be separate sentences. Consider the following two clauses:

➘   I will master English. I will complete every exercise in my textbook.

Either of these could become a time clause, and therefore make the main clause dependent on the timing of the other:

> ➘ I will master English **after** I complete every exercise in my textbook.
> ➘ **When** I master English, I will complete every exercise in my textbook.

Notice, however, that the time clause is no longer in the same tense as the main clause. Time clauses follow their own grammar rules.

Time Clause Rules

The patterns for forming time clauses are similar to regular clauses, with the same word order (except they start with an adverb), but time clauses use specific tenses.

When talking about past or present events, you can generally use the same tenses for time clauses.

> ➘ Before we cook pies, we wash our hands.
> ➘ He came home after he finished work.
> ➘ We ate dinner before we watched the movie.

Perfect tenses may be used to show further sequencing of time.

For the future, we use the present tenses to talk about future times:

> ➘ He will finish reading the book after he eats dinner. *(not* after he will eat dinner)
> ➘ They are going to the museum before we arrive. *(not* before we are going to arrive)
> ➘ I will practice my pronunciation until my friend's lesson has finished. *(not* until my friend's lesson will have finished)

As you can see in the examples above, when two clauses are joined by adverbs of time the future form should not be repeated.

> ↘ She will see me after it stops raining. *(not* after it will stop raining*)*
> ↘ I'll turn off my computer when he does. *(not* when he will do.*)*

Be careful, though, because the future tense may still be used if the time adverb introduces a noun clause. This happens when a clause is the object of a verb, and is not a time clause.

> ↘ I know when the boat will leave.
> ↘ They need to arrange a time when we will meet.

APPENDIX 4

BACKSHIFTING

Backshifting in English grammar is when a tense is shifted to the past (for instance from present to past). This usually happens in reported speech, or indirect speech, and can create quite complicated time structures, such as with the future in the past.

> ↘ I will go to the party.
> ↘ I said I would go to the party.

Backshifting can be applied to all tenses, when viewing an action or event from the past. A backshifted tense is usually introduced by a clause that indicates a past time. For example, a present tense statement reported in the past tense may be introduced with a past verb showing speech or thought.

> ↘ I like cupcakes.
> ↘ I **said** I liked cupcakes.
> ↘ We are going home.
> ↘ They **knew** we were going home.

With an introductory clause in the present, there is no need for a backshift.

> ↘ I think I like cupcakes.
> ↘ They know we are going home.

This table shows how each tense should be backshifted:

Example	Original Tense	Backshift to...	Backshift Example
I watch TV.	**Simple Present**	**Simple Past**	He knew I watched TV.
I wrote books.	**Simple Past**	**Past perfect**	It was true I had written books.
I have seen it all.	**Present Perfect**		I said I had seen it all.
I had studied hard.	**Past Perfect**		I thought I had studied hard.
I will win.	**will**	**would**	They predicted I would win.

Note that the past perfect does not change, as it cannot be shifted back further.

For progressive and perfect forms, auxiliary verbs should be backshifted as shown in this table:

Example	Original Tense	Backshift to...	Backshift Example
I am seeing her later.	**am / is / are**	**was / were**	I thought I was seeing her later.
It was getting dark.	**was / were**	**had**	I said it had been getting dark.
We have been here before.	**has / have**		The proved we had been there before.
What had been happening?	**had**		They asked what had been happening.

This can be used with the **going to** form for future, as you backshift **to be**.

➚ He is going to win the race.

➚ We thought he was going to win the race.

Note that when backshifting, depending on the context, you may also need to change expressions of time.

 ↘ "I am working today."
 ↘ I said I was working that day.

Expressions that show close proximity or time, such as **this, these** and **here** need to be changed to show distance (such as to **that, those** and **there**). Here are some examples of different expressions that need to change when backshifting, with ways to change them:

 ↘ now – then
 ↘ here – there
 ↘ this – that (*this morning* becomes *that morning*)
 ↘ these – those (*these days* becomes *those days*)
 ↘ today – that day
 ↘ tomorrow – the next (or following) day
 ↘ ago – before (*six months ago* becomes *six months before*)
 ↘ last week – the week before / the previous week
 ↘ next – the following (*next Tuesday* becomes *the following Tuesday*)

Lightning Source UK Ltd.
Milton Keynes UK
UKOW07f2357160217
294573UK00014B/119/P

9 780993 180804